THE

HISTORY

OF

FORGETTING

ALSO BY LAWRENCE RAAB

Visible Signs: New and Selected Poems

The Probable World

What We Don't Know About Each Other

Other Children

The Collector of Cold Weather

Mysteries of the Horizon

THE

HISTORY

OF

FORGETTING

LAWRENCE RAAB

PENGUIN POETS

PENGUIN BOOKS
Published by the Penguin Group
Penguin Group (USA) Inc., 375 Hudson Street, New York, New York 10014, U.S.A.
Penguin Group (Canada), 90 Eglinton Avenue East, Suite 700, Toronto, Ontario, Canada M4P 2Y3
(a division of Pearson Penguin Canada Inc.)
Penguin Books Ltd, 80 Strand, London WC2R 0RL, England
Penguin Ireland, 25 St Stephen's Green, Dublin 2, Ireland (a division of Penguin Books Ltd)
Penguin Group (Australia), 250 Camberwell Road, Camberwell, Victoria 3124, Australia
(a division of Pearson Australia Group Pty Ltd)
Penguin Books India Pvt Ltd, 11 Community Centre, Panchsheel Park, New Delhi – 110 017, India
Penguin Group (NZ), 67 Apollo Drive, Rosedale, North Shore 0632, New Zealand
(a division of Pearson New Zealand Ltd)
Penguin Books (South Africa) (Pty) Ltd, 24 Sturdee Avenue, Rosebank,
Johannesburg 2196, South Africa

Penguin Books Ltd, Registered Offices:
80 Strand, London WC2R 0RL, England

First published in Penguin Books 2009

1   3   5   7   9   10   8   6   4   2

Page vii constitutes an extension of this copyright page.

LIBRARY OF CONGRESS CATALOGING IN PUBLICATION DATA
Raab, Lawrence, 1946–
The history of forgetting / Lawrence Raab.
p. cm.—(Penguin poets)
ISBN 978-0-14-311582-3
I. Title.
PS3568.A2H57 2009
811'.54—dc22   2009002984

Printed in the United States of America
Set in Bembo
Designed by Ginger Legato

for my sister Susie

Acknowledgments

Grateful acknowledgment is made to the following magazines, in which some of these poems first appeared: *Bat City Review*, "The Uninvited"; *The Broome Review*, "The Afternoon Before We Met"; *Gastronomica*, "The First Still Life"; *The Georgia Review*, "Afloat" and "Twelfth Night"; *Gettysburg Review*, "True Paradises" and "Supernatural Forces"; *Gulf Coast*, "Mad Doctors" and "Recent Apparitions"; *The Idaho Review*, "Perhaps You've Heard This Story Before," "Blurred Snapshots," "Isn't It About Time," "Hurricane Season," and "Gratitude"; *Lake Effect*, "The Way They Lived Then," "Driving with Music," and "According to Freud"; *Margie*, "Domaine de la Solitude," "Even Clearer," "What God Must Have Known," and "Tenderness"; *New Ohio Review*, "The History of Forgetting," "Little Bird," and "The Weed Whacker Makes Me Yearn for the Scythe"; *The New Republic*, "Ecstatic"; *The New Yorker*, "Cruelty," "Hawthorne on His Way Home," "Mr. Fear," and "The Poem That Can't Be Written"; *The New York Times*, "The Invention of Nostalgia"; *Nightsun*, "The Reason Being" (as "Small Yellow Bird"), "A Friend's Umbrella," and "The Great Poem"; *Raritan*, "The God of Snow," "Likenesses," "The Origin of Surrealism," and "Adam's Dream"; *River City*, "Desire"; *River Styx*, "Three Wishes," "Another Theory About the Dinosaurs," and "Murdercycle"; *Solo Café*, "Against Compassion," "Once Something Must Have Happened Here," and "Sunday"; *Triquarterly*, "Faithless" and "Nothing There"; and *Washington Square*, "Sherlock Holmes Explains."

"The Great Poem" also appeared in *The Best American Poetry 2006*, edited by Billy Collins.

I would like to thank Yaddo, the Mellon Foundation, the Guggenheim Foundation, and Williams College for their generous support.

Contents

THE

HISTORY

OF

FORGETTING

1

The First Still Life

The scene at the table wasn't going well
so he thought, Why not try something
different? Leave Christ out. Do the bread
and wine by themselves. Add a knife.

Or perhaps the weather was bad—
had been for weeks—and the painter
of the first still life couldn't work outside
on his landscapes. Or he's poor

and can afford only small canvases
unsuited to a storm or crucifixion.
In front of him on the kitchen table:
a chipped white bowl and an apple.

He thinks, Take a bite out of it, call
the picture *Original Sin*. Or let the apple
decay, add a couple of flies, call it
Allegory of Life, or *Vanity*.

He understands that vanity and sin
will sell better than an apple in a bowl.
And yet—why not try the thing itself?
So he does. After which: blackberries

and lemons on a blue china plate,
peaches and grapes in a wicker basket,
a watermelon sliced open, then a trout,
then an eel, two glasses of wine

beside a letter on a desk, an egg in a cup.
And spoons and forks, of course, vases

of flowers, cascades of drapery. But first:
the apple in the bowl, a curve

of shadow on the top of the table.
He titles it *Apple in a Bowl*
to say: That's all that is here.
There's nothing you can't see.

A Friend's Umbrella

Ralph Waldo Emerson, toward the end
of his life, found the names
of familiar objects escaping him.
He wanted to say something about a window,
or a table, or a book on a table.

But the word wasn't there,
although other words could still suggest
the shape of what he meant.
Then someone, his wife perhaps,

would understand: "Yes, *window*! I'm sorry,
is there a draft?" He'd nod.
She'd rise. Once a friend dropped by
to visit, shook out his umbrella
in the hall, remarked upon the rain.

Later the word *umbrella*
vanished and became
the thing that strangers take away.

Paper, pen, table, book:
was it possible for a man to think
without them? To know
that he was thinking? *We remember
that we forget*, he'd written once,
before he started to forget.

Three times he was told
that Longfellow had died.

Without the past, the present

lay around him like the sea.
Or like a ship, becalmed,
upon the sea. He smiled

to think he was the captain then,
gazing off into whiteness,
waiting for the wind to rise.

Even Clearer

Don't be fooled by clarity,
there's always something behind it.
—DEAN YOUNG

Certain crimes are so clear
they'll never be understood.
The solution keeps opening into a past
so intricate and full of longing
even the most brilliant detective
finds himself lost. Look around.
Isn't everything a clue? The ringing
of a phone, the closing of a door,
a folded piece of paper. In Vienna
the young Hitler wanted to study art.
He painted pictures of cottages,
country roads, houses without people—
bad, yes, but not so bad, all things
considered, that he shouldn't have gotten
into art school. He'd have worked hard,
maybe stayed away from the beer halls,
then found a job teaching. Every day
a few billion histories fail to occur.
Many times the world has ended,
and many times things turned out
a lot better than they are right now.
Don't be fooled by what you can see.
Think back: the story of your life,
the one that happened, is enclosed
by the shadows of others,
every moment more deeply surrounded,
the way evening crosses a meadow
and climbs the walls of a house,
though inside a light still burns.

Cruelty

Vermont, 1965

That was the year my friends were reading
Antonin Artaud and Jean Genet.
The idea of cruelty felt important,
like being so perfect an outlaw
you became a saint. The war was on,
muffled, distant. Where we were
everything took place a few years later
than in New York or San Francisco.
Some would say it was too easy
for us to be there, talking
about almost anything. Too easy now
to say we didn't have a clue.
I made it through the first few chapters
of Artaud, and never got to *Saint Genet*,
although I remember the cover clearly,
the dome of his head, his eyes, the stare
that claimed he knew something
I would never know. My friends
moved on to de Sade. And now
it occurs to me that during all those years
I never said "I love you" to anyone,
although I probably should have lied
at least twice, to see if it was a lie.
Meanwhile, the fields and mountains promised
to remain the same, and they didn't.
Great poems told us that nature
would never betray us, but that really
wasn't the point, was it?
And then the theater of cruelty
stopped being shocking.
We all knew why.

True Paradises

The true paradises are the lost paradises.
—PROUST

It's the way the sentence unfolds—
true against lost, paradise
against paradise—that convinces the reader
and forbids contradiction. Yes, but now
I'm picturing certain students,
eager freshmen fiercely determined
to disagree, and one of them

has raised his hand. "I think," he says,
"that there are some true paradises
that don't have to be lost." "No,"
says Proust, "the true paradises
are the lost paradises." "Well," the student
continues, "isn't that just your point of view?
I mean, do we have to agree?" "Yes, you do,"

says Proust, obviously annoyed
and unaccustomed to the Socratic method.
"If you could hear the sentence,"
Proust explains, "which, clearly, you cannot,
you would understand it." "Well,"
says the student. "Sit down," says Proust,
and suddenly there are many hands, raised

and waving. The face of the great writer
clouds with distress, and he turns to me,
whose class this is, and says,
"They are all lost." I'm not sure
if he means the students or the paradises,
and I want to agree, but I'm feeling
a certain teacherly loyalty, luring me

into a thicket of qualifications. "Yes,"
I say, trying hard to sound ambiguous,
but for Proust the class is over.
He's at the door, fastening his cloak.
Then he turns back. "No matter," he says.
"Why should they believe it? What's lost,
what's true. Let them forget. Then remember."

Perhaps You've Heard This Story Before

It's the one where the king is out riding
through a dark forest and suddenly a witch
steps in front of his horse. The horse
rears up, but the king remains calm.
He knew that forest was haunted.
In those days, all the forests were haunted.

"What do you want, witch?"
he demands. And the witch says,
"Unless you return to this spot
within three days with the correct answer
to the following question, you will die."

No reason for this to be happening. No reason
why he's the one she stopped except
it was cool that morning inside her hovel,
so she walked out to stand in a patch
of sunlight, into which the king came riding.

"Three days," she cackles, repeating it
just for fun. "Then tell me the question,"
says the king, steadying his horse. You know
what happens next. The question's impossible.

The king searches night and day,
and everything he comes up with is wrong,
until by chance, at the last minute
he discovers the answer, gallops back,
tells the witch, and is saved.

Maybe the question was: What do women want?
Maybe something even harder. The point is,
there's an answer. That was the world
the king lived in, full of inexplicable dangers,

but at the end: certainty. That was why
the king could be brave and calm, and why

his horse, who wasn't able to think about danger
but felt it, needed to be steadied,
why the king touched her neck reassuringly,
then leaned down and spoke in her ear.
"There, there," he lied. "Nothing's wrong."

Tenderness

Brisbane hasn't called back
is the sentence a dream gave me.
Write it down, I was thinking,
when the dog jumped up on the bed,

which is what she likes to do an hour before
I need to be awake. She tucks herself
into my body, and once again
I'm wandering through the avenues of sleep.

So I lost that name. Somewhere
in Australia, I knew. Was it Sydney?
Perhaps a woman, then, angry
or hurt, unwilling to return my call?

No, she had to be a city,
out of touch with those who need
to hear from her, the way it happens
when the end of the world arrives.

London, Paris, Madrid—all the lines
are down. Now Brisbane
doesn't answer. Who's listening?
Maybe Gregory Peck in the submarine

from *On the Beach*. He's out tracking
a skittery noise, hoping that signal
from shore isn't the wind
fiddling with a telegraph key.

But it is. And soon, all over Australia,
the streets are empty, no bodies
on the sidewalks, no blood, no trace
of us beyond what we built. Death,

in this movie, has gone inside
and closed the doors, although
in the version I'm imagining
birds still dart and swoop through the air.

Butterflies glide from flower to flower.
Only the dogs, having survived
their masters, seem confused.
Let them hop back up on those unmade beds

and feel, for a day or two, bereft,
before they learn again the ways of wolves
and say goodbye to tenderness,
or what we thought was tenderness.

Desire

for Jonathan Aaron

It was late, and I was trying to remember
what someone once said about our woes—
how they rise out of our unwillingness
to stay in our rooms. After which
I opened the window, and both of us heard
the rustling sounds outside, as if small
furtive things were hurrying away, or hiding.
You were reminded of the movie *Frogs*
in which one character after another unwisely
leaves the house only to be hunted down
by animals not generally known
for deliberate acts of revenge.
Thus proving that what we do to the world
returns to haunt us. Radioactivity,
I said, is the usual explanation.
Also carelessness, greed, and desire.
Maybe, you replied. But Ava Gardner
was the most beautiful woman who ever lived.
There can be no doubt about that.
Although Grace Kelly in *Rear Window*
comes very close, for different reasons.
That left us silent and transfixed.
Outside, something was moving around,
something which now seemed
to have found its way into the walls.

Afloat

After the interesting guest at the party
declared that Giorgione's *The Storm*
was the strangest painting ever made,
you flew to Venice to see it. And the canals
as well, the celebrated light
on the water, all those churches
where someone might be playing Bach
or Vivaldi while off in a shadowy corner
another masterpiece begs to be discovered.
So, for a time, yours is a life
of important surprises. You'd like
to forget that Venice is sinking
and no one knows how to save it, but today
walking across the flooded piazza feels
almost instructive: the mortal
just touching our need for permanence.
So much, after all, is vanishing.
And still the delicate city remains afloat,
the water you don't want to fall into
glittering cheerfully as you cross the bridge
to the Accademia, where at last you will find
the enigmatic *Tempesta*, a picture much admired
by Byron, who in general detested painting
unless it could remind him
of something he had seen
or some day might see.

Mad Doctors

Even as children they always went too far.
What will happen, they kept thinking,
if I pull that switch, strike this match?
Maybe no one told them not to,
or explained, logically, what could go wrong.
Then they were playing with lightning,

wondering what they would do if they didn't
have to die. Consider Doctor Cyclops,
stuck in the middle of the jungle
with his radium, making things small.

It's 1940, five years before Hiroshima.
Even then science wasn't on our side.
In the movie, Albert Dekker's
shaved head makes him monstrous
and impressive, and a little like a child.
Yet he seems to have no past—

no wife to bring back from the dead,
no motive for evil, nothing but research.
His eyes are bad and he hardly sleeps.
We should remember Doctor Cyclops

from time to time, and Doctor Frankenstein,
Doctor Jekyll, and Doctor X.
They were all deceived by ambition,
although they believed themselves
betrayed by the world.

Maybe no one ever told them
we don't need to live forever.
Maybe no one explained, exactly,
the logic of it.

The History of Forgetting

When Adam and Eve lived in the garden
they hadn't yet learned how to forget.
For them every day was the same day.
Flowers opened, then closed.
They went where the light told them to go.
They slept when it left, and did not dream.

What could they have remembered,
who had never been children? Sometimes
Adam felt a soreness in his side,
but if this was pain it didn't appear
to require a name, or suggest the idea
that anything else might be taken away.
The bright flowers unfolded,
swayed in the breeze.

It was the snake, of course, who knew
about the past—that such a place could exist.
He understood how people would yearn
for whatever they'd lost, and so to survive
they'd need to forget. Soon
the garden will be gone, the snake
thought, and in time God himself.

These were the last days—Adam and Eve
tending the luxurious plants, the snake
watching from above. He knew
what had to happen next, how persuasive
was the taste of that apple. And then
the history of forgetting would begin—
not at the moment of their leaving,
but the first time they looked back.

The Way They Lived Then

Beginning with a phrase by
Georg Christoph Lichtenberg

In former days when the soul
was still immortal, men and women walked
beside the sea, in and out of the fog, talking

as we might talk today, the fog
wrapped around them, then rising,
their hands apart, then touching.

How changed is the world
from the one they never doubted?
Each night the news informs us.

What once was vast
will be small, what was endless
will end. After which:

black holes, burnt-out stars
wandering through the dark.
We won't be there, you and I.

But can't you hear, stepping
outside, in the sound of water
or of birds, some diminishment?

Remember the past? The way they lived then?
What they took for granted?
What they didn't have to understand?

Hawthorne on His Way Home

Walking through the village
of Danvers, late one afternoon
in the fall of 1836, Nathaniel Hawthorne
saw an old man carrying

two dry, rustling bundles
of cornstalks, and he thought:
A good personification of Autumn.
Another man was hoeing up potatoes.

What did he represent? It was October.
The wild rosebushes were bare.
In the fields—brittle Indian corn,
pale rows of cabbages.

"A landscape now wholly autumnal,"
Hawthorne wrote in his journal, and perhaps
he noticed the way *now* means *then*
as soon as it's written down,

the way remembering conceals invention,
or tries to. Idea for a tale:
a man, composing a story, finds
it shaping itself against his intentions.

The characters act otherwise
than he planned. Unforeseen events occur.
Hawthorne paused. Above the village
clouds were being carried off by the wind.

In a story, he thought, what a man observes
might shadow forth his fate:
wild roses, barberry, Indian corn.
The down of thistles flying through the air.

$$\underline{2}$$

Mr. Fear

He follows us, he keeps track.
Each day his lists are longer.
Here, death. And here,
something like it.

Mr. Fear, we say in our dreams,
what do you have for me tonight?
And he looks through his sack,
his black sack of troubles.

Maybe he smiles when he finds
the right one. Maybe he's sorry.
Tell me, Mr. Fear,
what must I carry

away from your dream?
Make it small, please.
Let it fit in my pocket,
let it fall through

the hole in my pocket.
Fear, let me have
a small brown bat
and a purse of crickets

like the ones I heard
singing last night
out there in the stubbly field
before I slept, and met you.

Recent Apparitions

One day someone looked up and saw it—
not the dirty window it had been
for five years after the seal broke,
three floors up in a brick wall
in the Milton Hospital in Massachusetts,

not just that cloudy pane of glass
but the Virgin Mary, head bowed in sorrow.
Within a week twenty-five thousand people
arrived to see her. A boy in a wheelchair
touched the wall with his legs,

but didn't walk away. His mother wept.
Many left flowers. A man from Florida,
who had recognized the Virgin once before
in the window of an insurance company
in Clearwater, said, "Whether or not

it's a true apparition, it's a sign to us."
For a day or two the story gets in the papers.
Then the figure starts to change
and the crowds thin out. Soon
it's only a broken window except to those

who want to remember, maybe wonder
how long she might have been there
before anyone noticed. Perhaps
every window contains a secret apparition.
Perhaps the world is full of signs,

and if we looked around we'd see things
as they really are—not just a stony hillside
and a tree, not just the bitter rain,
or that trail of smoke
always disappearing into the sky.

Another Theory About the Dinosaurs

Just because they're dead doesn't mean
they were failures. The dinosaurs,
after all, had their 120 million years.
To end it, a giant meteor came along.
Or else God decided he wanted to try
something different for a while:
smaller animals, more men and women.

It must have been good
to have been an American and believed
in the West. Endless space. The Open Road.
You shot buffalo from the train
just to watch them fall. You blasted away
at the clouds of birds because the gun
felt right against your shoulder.

Even better to have been certain
God cared for you the way he didn't
care for others. So if someone
poured molten lead down your throat,
or set a pile of sticks beneath
your feet on fire, you knew the future
was on your side. Back then

only the poor cared about the poor
and no one thought about the dinosaurs,
how one day they'd be so famous
vast rooms would be constructed
to contain their bones and display
cunning models rearing high above us—
huge, fierce, doomed—
more like gods than ancestors.

After We Saw What There Was to See

After we saw what there was to see
we went off to buy souvenirs, and my father
waited by the car and smoked. He didn't need
a lot of things to remind him where he'd been.
Why do you want so much stuff?
he might have asked us. "Oh, *Ed*," I can hear
my mother saying, as if that took care of it.

After she died I don't think he felt any reason
to go back through all those postcards, not to mention
the glossy booklets about the Singing Tower
and the Alligator Farm, the painted ashtrays
and lucite paperweights, everything we carried home
and found a place for, then put away
in boxes, then shoved far back in our closets.

He'd always let my mother keep track of the past,
and when she was gone—why should that change?
Why did I want him to need what he'd never needed?
I can see him leaning against our yellow Chrysler
in some parking lot in Florida or Maine.
It's a beautiful cloudless day. He glances at his watch,
lights another cigarette, looks up at the sky.

Two Instances of Looking Back

1

You want a last glimpse of your house—
that makes sense. The city's on fire,
you're clutching a bundle of clothes,
a few pots and pans—battered, heavy—
not much to save. Yes, the angels
said God said not to look back.
But wasn't that metaphorical?
Meaning: Let the past go. Trust me.
One glance, one small disobedience
you wouldn't have scolded your child for,
and there you are: the residuum
of a million tears, for a moment taking
the form of a woman raising her hand
as if in farewell, or surprise.

2

You win her back from death with beauty
and lose her before you get home.
Hades told you not to look back,
but why? Because he knew you would?
Because that's how this becomes
a memorable story? Some say you forgot,
or grew anxious. (She was so quiet.
Was she really there?) Then you turned,
and she raised her hand as if
you could grasp it and save her. Or else
she was surprised—what were you doing?
Then all that darkness swept her away,
and because you were still alive
you went on, for a while, being alive.

Driving with Music

Idling in traffic, bass jacked
all the way up, the car shuddering,
the driver pretending not to notice,
his friends nodding to the beat—how easy
it is to hate them when you're standing
out in the sun on the sidewalk, or some
country road in early spring. And then
you're the one in the car.
A song takes you back, lets you touch
what you couldn't reach in silence.
Which means the song should be played

again and louder, as if that were the way
to live with disappointment. Perhaps
the soul is divided like this,
half desiring to hear itself listening,
half needing to be seized
and overwhelmed. And each remains fearful
of the other, the one who might
at any moment do something foolish—
the way a man suddenly drives
his car off the road, while someone else
just stands there and watches it happen.

According to Freud

there are no accidents,
though it could take years
of talk to figure out why. Meanwhile,
your wife has left you. She didn't need
to be sure. According to her,

there are only accidents—
the allure of secrets, then nothing
but the shabby appearances of order.
So today you believe in fate,
tomorrow in freedom. The curse is Greek

and absolute. Follow that road far enough
and you have to tear your eyes out because
you can't bear to see the day
you've spent your life trying to avoid
and crawling toward. It's enough

to drive you crazy, and you feel like
tearing your eyes out all over again.
According to Freud, that story
conceals another, the one in which
every son needs to take his father's place.

Nor is the father innocent.
Nor the wife who doesn't want
to think about it. Nor the world
in which a man can make these things up,
as if behind the accidents of life

were the quarrels of gods. And this,
according to Freud, reminds us
of something else, once familiar,
but now so far away
we have to die to get there.

Faithless

The tide is full, the moon lies fair
Upon the straits . . .

—MATTHEW ARNOLD

By mid-July I'm tired of the mountains.
I want to be near the sea,
walk beside it for an hour or two,
watch it cleaning the wounds of the shore.
Such persistence—though we know
there isn't a plan, just this
going back over the same places,
revising everything out.
"Is there a way to win?"
Jane Greer asks Robert Mitchum
in *Out of the Past.* "Well," he says,
"there's a way to lose more slowly."
He knows he shouldn't trust her,
and he doesn't care. Ah, Matthew Arnold,
our lovers are more melancholy than yours,
more desperate, more faithless.
"You can't help anything you do,"
Mitchum tells her at the end.
Which is what he might have told himself.
But nobody ever sees how far
the things we shouldn't feel can take us.
I just want to walk along the shore
for an hour, watch the waves
rearranging whatever they can.
I like the way the sea encourages me
to think about the past,
as if I could leave it where it is:
the moon on the water, the stars
that gleam and are gone.

Blurred Snapshots

1

Somebody moved. Somebody didn't
want his picture taken. So he's fooling around,
ruining things for everyone else. But sometimes
it's the mother, the one with the camera,

whose hand shakes and slides them all
out of focus, along with a lake or a mountain,
and usually, beside them, a large plaque
that would have explained where they were.

2

I don't often look at the albums of snapshots
my mother so carefully put together.
The oldest, the most beautiful, have black pages
she used white ink to write on—places
and dates, but sometimes a comment:
"Wonderful summer!" Or: "Larry's first fish!"

Black and white is the way to see the past.
When she turns to color, everything becomes
a little garish and unreal.
Summer vacations, birthdays and Christmas
are the books' important subjects, the plot
that moves us from season to season, during which
we get more presents and grow older.

3

Frequently, along the way, we climb out
of the car to admire the view, a mountain
for example, the upper ledges of which

resemble the head of an Indian chief.
Then we have our picture taken beside the plaque.

"See the Indian," my mother's written
in the album, and yes, off in the blur
of distance, there he is: a stern profile
staring enigmatically to the left,
as if down the road we arrived on.

And there we are, my sister, my father,
and me, gazing into the camera.
Since we never asked strangers to help,
one of us is always missing.

    4

I believe my mother often looked
at these books by herself. Perhaps
they made her feel sad, and perhaps
that's what she wanted to feel.

So many blurred pictures.
She wouldn't throw anything away,
even if she knew we'd never
find the time to go through it all.

But we could. That was the point.
That was why you saved things.
Because as soon as it's gone,
my mother said, you'll want it back.

    5

Somebody moved. Somebody's always
horsing around, refusing to smile,
pretending he has to escape.

Stand still, she says.
This won't take a minute.

They're posing beside another monument,
a man on a horse with a sword,
or they're leaning against a boulder,
then kneeling at the edge of the ocean.
Now they're in front of their house.

It's Christmas. There's the tree,
the bright circle of presents.
Someday, their mother is thinking,
they'll have all of these pictures to look at
whenever they want to remember.

This makes her happy, and she takes another
shot of the tree, which every year she says
is the most beautiful tree they've had.
And why not? she thinks. Why can't that be true?

Three Wishes

It's too easy, isn't it,
to imagine almost anything these days.
Think about "weapons of mass destruction,"
for example, the movies that start running
in your mind, then the actual pictures.
Sometimes the expected losses include us all.
Once . . . but how would we know
what once was like? Once a trip of a few miles
might have turned into a grand adventure.
Once you could believe in the soul.

But now, anyone who asks
if you've put your trust in a personal savior
is someone you shouldn't let into your house.
He goes next door. He knows you're doomed.
Yesterday, I found a crumpled piece of paper
out in the woods—three holes, blue lines
to write on, and a single sentence
crossed out several times:
You can make your life better by
Maybe the writer couldn't decide
what "better" meant. More meaningful?
More fun? Even in a fairy tale
it doesn't work out. You have to use
the third wish to undo the second,
which means you get nothing,
which was what you had to begin with.

And since you're a poor fisherman
in this version of the story,
you end up hungry and alone,
staring off at the sea. How good it was,

the story wants you to think,
to have been content
with so little. How clear the future
used to look, how hard to imagine
anything could change.

The Afternoon Before We Met

If the afternoon had been blue,
there might have been less desire.
—CARLOS DRUMMOND DE ANDRADE

If the sky had been clear,
if the water had been colder,
if the music had continued, perhaps
we wouldn't have fallen in love.

Was the afternoon blue?
But we hadn't met that afternoon.
It was gray, it was no color at all
since we were only about to meet.

The trees kept to themselves,
they were the same trees they'd been
all summer, just waiting
to be given their roles in the scene

we'd soon enter, desire about
to press our hands together, to whisper
in a way we hadn't heard it whisper
that afternoon, or any other day.

In Praise of Worry

Think of it and it won't happen,
I've often thought. Too unlikely
to imagine the accident—you
in the car in the rain—then receive
the call. Too uncanny,
too much like a book.

In life, almost no one
recognizes what's important
when it's beginning—the comical bully
on his way to power, the shy boy
next door loading his gun, or the baby
in the barn, only the animals watching.

Then a few travelers arrive in the night.

Later, we can see the shape of the story,
or make one up, if we have to.

So you're driving home in a terrible storm.
Rain lashes the windshield, great trees
are collapsing, but you're safe
because the scene I'm picturing

won't happen if I think of it first.
That's what I keep telling myself
until the storm is over—
challenging the order of things
to show its hand, betting it won't.

The Invention of Nostalgia

Before 1688 nostalgia didn't exist.
People felt sad and thought about home,
but in 1688 Johannes Hofer, a Swiss doctor,
came up with the word. It wasn't
what he himself was feeling, but a malady

he'd observed in soldiers along the frontier.
Leeches and opium were the cures,
and if those failed, a return to the Alps.
Therefore: homesickness, nostalgia's symptom,
the way your stomach felt that first night

at summer camp, though if you cried
so hard you had to leave, later
you probably found yourself thinking,
They're swimming now, they're having lunch.
And you felt sad in a different way.

Imagine those soldiers sent back
to their mountains, some of them wondering
why they're not happy. How much it hurts
to want what's gone, all those days
that have left their cloudy pictures in our minds,

and the smell of certain rooms, the light
through trees at certain hours—that time
before the first time we felt it,
like all the years before 1688
when no one had the right word to turn to.

Regret

Every day there's something old
to feel sorry about—
what I should have done and didn't,
or what I did, and kept on doing.

I want to believe
everyone's forgotten by now.
Then I picture them thinking back.

And those who've died
and earned the wisdom death allows
just shake their heads and sigh.
"Very funny," my father would say

after my sister and I played
some cruel little joke on him.
"Ha, ha," he'd add,
to let us know he got the point.

We want to forget
until we start to forget.
We want the past to change,
and we want it back.

"Enough is enough,"
my father used to say
to tell us it was over.

Ecstatic

Nine months to a year
was what the doctors gave my friend.
All summer he said he felt *ecstatic*.
That was his word. No, he hadn't

fallen in love with death.
Ecstatic was the way he thought
the world wanted him to feel—
trees swaying as he sat on his deck,

crickets in the grass, then the moon
coming out. They were all part of how
this was happening. Two months later,
when the serious pain set in,

he said he'd been wrong. *Deluded*
was his word. But why shouldn't
a man who knows he's going
to die believe he's found

some new kind of truth?
Then pain makes itself the truth.
Try to fool yourself now, it says.
Try to believe in anything but me.

Supernatural Forces

"The absence of God," wrote Georges Bataille,
"is greater, and more divine, than God."
Which is an idea God might have come up with
if he'd been French and worried
about how to make it through
the twentieth century. Do you want this?
If I take it away, will you want it more?

Or will you forget? That's the problem
with absence, it leaves itself open
to so much. Supernatural forces,
for example. Glowing lights,
out of which the aliens appear
like anorexic children. Let us help you,
they say, although of course they never speak.

Once they just wanted to take over the planet.
Now they feel sorry for us,
the way God must have felt when he chose
to retire into his silence.
No more threats. No more angels, either.
Only these lost children, come back
to startle us, and vanish.

3

The Poem That Can't Be Written

is different from the poem
that is not written, or the many

that are never finished—those boats
lost in the fog, adrift

in the windless latitudes,
the charts useless, the water gone.

In the poem that cannot
be written there is no danger,

no ponderous cargo of meaning,
no meaning at all. And this

is its splendor, this is how
it becomes an emblem,

not of failure or loss,
but of the impossible.

So the wind rises. The tattered sails
billow, and the air grows sweeter.

A green island appears.
Everyone is saved.

Lucky for Us

Most books say the sun is a star. But it still knows
how to change back into the sun in the daytime.
  —FROM A STUDENT PAPER

Lucky for us things know what they know.
Most books say the earth is round,
but it knows how to be flat when it has to.
And when I drive over to your house,
I'm not afraid of planets or stars

crashing into me, because there are laws
that say they can't. Thanks to gravity
we don't spin out of control, rise into
the air, or just float away. No fair
jumping up, gravity says, without coming down.

No fair running without getting tired,
or knowing how you feel without saying it.
There are laws for every part of the day—
invisible laws for what we can't touch,
laws for the night. Look at the clouds—

what are they up to? Just circling the earth,
blocking the light, making us all tired and low.
Why does anything need more than one name?
We don't have to think about breathing to breathe.
It's one of those smart things our bodies do

without being asked. Most books
will tell you this, if you have to read it.
Before Copernicus, the sun wasn't even a star.
Before Galileo, no one could see the moon.
Before I met you, I was blind.

Flowering Pear

The Taoist master Chuang Tzu dreamt he was
a butterfly. When he woke he wondered,
Was I a man dreaming I was a butterfly,
or am I a butterfly who dreams he is a man?

It's beautiful—the way likeness
keeps itself aloft, refusing
to settle for long on a plum branch,
for example, where now the butterfly
is folding its brilliant wings,

or on the shore of a lake in autumn
where a man is watching the moon as it rises—
first in the sky, then in the water.

Tonight, when I dream,
I'd like the comfort of the rain
to keep me from waking.
Then, in the morning, I might not remember

where I went, or what I turned into,
how I was afraid, perhaps,
or how I'd forgotten what it was like
to be afraid. I can see myself

throwing the covers off
without regret. Oblivious,
I'll grind the coffee,
glance at the sparrows on the lawn.
But later, settling down at my desk,

surely I'll be lured into wondering
why anything is itself when it could be
a flowering pear, or a hawk, or a man
at his desk in the morning—not me,
but someone I might become.

The Origin of Surrealism

The life of the Japanese beetle
is pointless and ugly. That's what I'm thinking
as I flick a few of them off the zinnias
and into a can—not enough
to make a difference,
only the smallest kind of satisfaction.
Now I'm wondering if these grim ideas

might lead me somewhere. So I sit down
at my typewriter and the dog next door
begins to bark. He barks just long enough
to transform the silence that follows
into the moment before his barking
will begin again. I stare at the page and wait.
Then somebody turns a radio on, and I know

I have to be in a completely different place,
maybe Paris in the twenties, a small café
where only artists gather. We work
all night, smoke and drink all afternoon,
and talk about beauty, and chance,
and beauty again. When a dog barks,
it's the beginning of a necessary thought.
When a few bars of music float by,
that's just what we need.

Today we've been examining our dreams,
taking for granted the amazing
afternoon light of Paris as it drifts
through the swirls of smoke above us.
Across the table, André Breton
stubs out his cigarette and leans toward me,
his way of saying it's my turn to speak.

"The whole ridiculous life," I begin,
"of the Japanese beetle is completely
devoted to the creation of ugliness."
André smiles, as if he knows exactly
what I mean. Then he lights another cigarette,
and gazes into the future. "Yes," he declares.
"Nothing but the astonishing is beautiful."

Women at Twilight

A woman is sneaking out of town
to meet the devil. She's young
and so lovely she has no idea
how lovely she is.

He knows. They've met already
in the gloomy woods. She thought
she'd gone to gather sticks,
but really she was wandering

far away from home.
"You're not surprised to see me,"
he says. All the leaves tremble
when the wind passes through.

Women at twilight, slipping out
of their houses, lost in the forest,
afraid of their hearts—this
used to happen all the time.

What did they want?
How much did they remember?
"Hush," he says.
"You don't have to answer."

What God Must Have Known

Pandora was one of many
fallible women set up for a fall,
another Eve who couldn't
keep her hands to herself. Of course
the gods knew she'd open that box.

They were always having fun,
showing off and screwing around.
Curiosity was the only motivation
they gave her, so she did
what she had to—let the troubles loose.

Hard to imagine Zeus wasn't pleased
with this little machine of a play.
Or that God hadn't known
from the beginning that Eve
would eat that apple. Did he really

hope she'd surprise him?—
he who couldn't help but see
the end of the future.
If only he'd had a few friends
to confide in, joke around with.

But God was always so serious.
No pranks in this story—
just disappointment, then anger.
Of course we would hurt him.
Like every father, he'd shown us how.

The Uninvited

There are two ghosts in the house
Ray Milland and his sister
move into at the beginning
of the movie. They don't know this,
and they're both skeptical
when things start happening—the sound
of weeping before dawn, the room their dog
refuses to enter, that elusive scent of mimosa.
It's all pretty tame by today's standards,
where you can count on somebody
getting a spike through her head as soon
as she's had sex with her boyfriend. But in 1944
you had time to be unsettled.
There were good mothers and bad ones,
and it took a while to figure that out.
Then you looked back at your life
and saw how the pieces fit together—
why there was weeping, and what made it stop.
So the past isn't over until we understand it,
which is one of the reasons
ghosts keep appearing. They need us to see
who they were, and sometimes
they won't rest until they believe
we forgive them.

Once Something Must Have Happened Here

Everything would have been different—
the sound of the trees, the face of the moon,
the light. The light especially—
it would have surprised us, demanded
that we pay attention to whatever was happening.
Were there more than two people involved?
Was there a child? Was the child hidden,
but watching? Perhaps the trees interfered,

and as the moon rose, fantastic shadows
were cast on the lawn. Perhaps,
from inside the woods, there was the call
of a bird that should not, at that hour,
have been singing. Or else:
no forest, only a few low bushes
with thorns and inedible berries, poor land
that required all their attention,

so at night they were too tired to dream.
Or they dreamt, but could not remember.
Later, no one wanted to remember,
which is why we know so little.
Nor does it seem right, now,
to make something up so we can pretend
to understand, and say how much they were like us,
or how different, how impossible to understand.

Likenesses

Like a town called Shade Gap, or Burnt Cabins,
one of those places where the past
keeps threatening to vanish.
Like this man, a stranger, just lying there
on his side in the street, as if he wanted
to prove something. And like a book
in which such things must have reasons
behind them. So the end of a story looks back
at the way it began. And when that stranger
refuses to speak, it's part of a shape
we weren't ready to notice. Like the crowd
that gathers around him, expectant,
then confused. Like the remains
of a cabin far out in the hills.
No one recalls the people who lived there,
why they lived there. In the book
only their absence is important.
Like the sound of a branch falling
on a windy night. Like the way we return
in dreams to the houses
we grew up in—maybe a sliver
of moon in the bedroom window,
maybe a light under the door.

Sunday

So that's life, then: things as they are?
—WALLACE STEVENS

Once there was music that could tear
your heart open and heal it
before you took another breath.
That was what art could do.
Kings and princes, bishops and popes

all knew this, as they knew
how to get what they wanted and keep
what they had. Mostly what happens
to people doesn't happen by chance.
You spend your life in the mud,

you eat the same thin soup each night,
and then on Sunday a thousand angels
start to sing. The walls are ablaze
with suffering and forgiveness.
And you think this is what you'll see

when you die. When you yearn,
this is what you yearn for. Or something
like it, the version you've been told
you can afford. They were smart to keep
belief and understanding at a distance,

go for the big effects, everything you get
when you're through with this world,
the one you got stuck with—potatoes and soup,
the morning and the afternoon,

the afternoon and the evening,
things as they are.

Murdercycle

(1999, Horror)

An alien motorcycle roars into town
on a mission to kill. That's how
TV Guide explains it, leaving open the question
of whether it's one of ours, say a Harley
or BMW, or one of those bikes designed
by and for aliens. In either case,

the bike arrives around noon, stops in front
of the post office, and revs itself up.
Maybe it's searching for someone
in particular—a scientist, perhaps.
Maybe it's just eager to kill.

Back in the lab, that scientist's pretty daughter
is worrying again about her father's health.
"Slow down, Dad," she keeps telling him,
but he knows there's too much to do,
too little time. Meanwhile, on Main Street,
their handsome lab assistant

is getting nervous as he watches
the bike rear up and head out of town. "Cool!"
a kid exclaims. "I don't like the look of that,"
an old man mutters, and someone says
they should call the sheriff, but won't he

just laugh at this foolishness?
Not when he sees it for himself. That's the way
the story unfolds—from doubt
to amazement, from a normal Saturday afternoon
when nobody is expecting to die, to a Sunday
or Monday when half the town's in flames.

It doesn't take long for people to reveal
everything they've worked hard to keep hidden.
Some are the cowards, many are selfish,
but a few will surprise themselves
by their determination, or their kindness,

and they'll be rewarded
with their lives, as they would not
in a different kind of movie, one that took
the world more seriously, and refused
to acknowledge such ludicrous
and impossible situations as these.

Sherlock Holmes Explains

Never trust general impressions, old chap.
Concentrate on the details. I always look
at a woman's sleeves first.
—Sherlock Holmes

I could tell you what it means
if a button is undone. I could explain
exactly, in this case for example,

when I knew. Remember the way
she knocked on our door? Which chair
she sat in? How she stirred her tea?

Details connect, and the plot unfolds.
She hasn't noticed the button
missing from her sleeve.

But she's certain she understands
what we think of her, which is how
she'll give herself away, and why

we must train ourselves
not to be deceived. You will learn
to confide in us, I said.

And she replied, Oh, but I have!
Remember that, Watson?
Then she smiled, and raised

her hand to her throat to touch
the necklace she wasn't wearing.
That was when I knew.

The God of Snow

The crisp snow made a pleasant crunching
sound under our feet as we walked; and it
occurred to me to say: "O Kinjurō, is there
a God of Snow?"

—LAFCADIO HEARN

O Kinjurō, I said, is there also
a God of Rain, a God of Wind, a God
for every day of the week? But first,
Kinjurō, tell me about the ghostly foxes
and the shadowy children. Where
do they live? How do they speak?

He laughed. So many questions!
Why not open your eyes? So I told him
that in my country it's unfair
to answer a question with a question,
and he gave me a narrow look, as though
the time for banter had passed.

Yes, I can still see that look. And then
it started to snow. Our footsteps filled
quickly. The light dimmed. Travel became
more taxing. Wasn't it time to turn back?
But Kinjurō seemed intent on pressing ahead.
Where are we going, Kinjurō? I implored.

Each must determine his own path,
he called through the thickening snow.
I wanted to explain that I didn't mean
in life, I meant *right at that moment*

in the storm, in that town
of wherever we were, on a morning

I was certain had begun so pleasantly.
At least, that's what I remember thinking—
that it had all started out so well.

Domaine de la Solitude

A Côtes du Rhône, 2001, and very good
for $8.99 on sale—naturally I bought it
for the name. How could I resist
tasting the domain of solitude?
Of the Lançon family, whose domain this is,
I know only that for five centuries

generation after generation
has committed itself to cultivating
the particular grapes that have,
pampered and transformed, filled
this now empty bottle. I feel

they should have charged more.
Of course this may be their budget line,
developed by the younger family members
and scorned by Monsieur Lançon himself,
who sees in this vintage, which he will not
consent to taste, nothing less

than the end of civilization.
Values, honor, breeding—all lost, all sold
to the rabble just to pay the taxes
on the château, which now he can hardly
bear to live in. He's moved

to the bedroom overlooking the garden,
away from the vineyard.
He no longer talks to his son.
Sometimes, however, it pleases him
to observe little Henri
when the boy wanders into the garden,

tossing his red ball high in the air
and hardly ever catching it, so it falls
among the flowers, crushing them.
Then Monsieur Lançon must try very hard
not to rap sharply on the window

to tell that careless child to stop.
Doesn't he see what he's doing?
Hasn't anyone taught him how
to catch a ball? A simple thing like that!
Why must you torment your grandfather, Henri?
Now go away. Stop crying, but go away.

Against Compassion

After he wrote "Against Compassion," the poem
all agree defined his career, and made him
famous in those circles where poetry can do
that sort of thing, after he replied, sometimes
at extravagant length, to the messages

of shock *The New Yorker* forwarded,
and corrected the few who praised him
for his irony, insisting he was a poet who believed
everything he said—after that he decided
to write "In Praise of Death." It was too easy.

There were so many good arguments already.
"Against Love" followed, and he felt the same
loss of confidence. Could any way
of avoiding pain be dismissed? Sympathy,
pity, even vengeance: slippery slopes

in them all. Then stupidity and ignorance—
oh, they were too much fun to embrace.
Why was it so hard to be purely wrong?
How had he managed it even once? That was when
he sat down in front of the beautiful window

of the little house in the woods he'd built
with the Guggenheim money, watched the trees
he didn't know the names of posing in the sunlight,
the ferns tucked away in the shady corners,
and the squirrels, birds, and caterpillars

all going about their business unaware
of his interest, and that was when he wrote
"Why I Love Everything in the World,"
which most agree defined the second half
of his sadly brief career.

Taking Out the Moon

Oh, there are always ideas, he'd admit.
But after a while it's just tiring
to line up the words on the page

and cross the wrong ones out,
find a better adjective than "pale,"
a livelier noun than "sadness."

Are there too many poems about the moon?
Probably. But will anyone notice
one more? And even if love

and solitude are themes
that can't be exhausted, it would still
be fatiguing—all the afternoons of nothing

but words, followed by evenings
of more of the same. And then the next day:
the need to look back, take out the moon,

add a bicycle, a handkerchief, the dawn.

The Great Poem

The great poem is always possible.
Think of Keats and his odes.
But we shouldn't have to be dying.

What I'm writing now is not
the great poem. After a few lines
I could tell. It may not even be

a particularly good poem, although
it's too early to decide about that.
Keep going, I say. See what happens.

But trying hard is one of the problems,
since it shows in the lines as a strain
or struggle that reminds the reader

too much of the writer, whereas
most readers want to listen alone.
The great poem, I think, will arrive

when I no longer care. Perhaps
I'll have abandoned art altogether,
and I won't even want to write

the poem down. But then I'll remember
what I once would have given
for this moment, and I'll go back

to my desk. And I'll write the poem
as though I were another person,
someone I will never be again.

4

Invisible Music

Where are the songs of Spring? Aye,
where are they?

—KEATS

This day, I've decided,
is for answerable questions only.
Nothing about death, or the silence of God,
nothing even about the chance of life
on some faraway planet, or the future of ours.
Nothing at all concerning the future—

what we have to plan for, what we don't want
to think about. Not this morning,
which is sunny and calm, weather
that will continue through the afternoon
and into the evening, followed by a 20% chance
of rain after midnight, but even then

only showers, no high winds,
large hail, or frequent lightning,
no possibility at all of a tornado
or one of those sudden climate changes
that ushers in a new ice age, completely
rearranging life as we know it. Today

is a day for life as we know it,
for everything predictable and clearly defined,
any question the dictionary can answer,
like the meaning of *descant*, or *apocrypha*,
or the difference between a frieze
and a relief. Whatever its name,

that's what I've been looking at: a dozen
pale singers in Grecian attire, two young men
playing some sort of trumpet, and in the center

four large children kicking up their heels—
one dimension pushing itself out
into three, and getting halfway there.

What are they celebrating? Something gone,
something over. As this morning
almost is. In the park, a few families
have spread blankets under the trees.
They're eating sandwiches, reading the paper.
Two dogs are romping. And now

the laughter of the children
rises above the voices of their parents,
and the water in the fountain
glitters and dances, as if
to invisible music, which I can
almost hear, almost see the shape of.

Four Explanations

Explanations come to an end somewhere.
— WITTGENSTEIN

Some were born with wings.
You had to walk. So the story went.
Some were told what to expect.
You were given riddles.
To all of them "man" was the answer.
Which meant you were back
where you started, one foot
in the grave, one hand gesturing
wildly at the sky.

This was enough
to require another explanation: the one
about why you might decide
to climb the stairs, enter the room,
and open the window. The one
about what happens
if you leap out—how the air
will refuse to hold you.

Any kind of thinking,
you once supposed, could blossom
into another, the way logic concedes
to surprise, the way love
just smiles at the labors of reason.
Now you're older. You take
your child, your wayward child,
aside and say, I don't want to hear
any more explanations.
Tell me the truth.

The world is an accident,
or it isn't. Everything you count on

is taken away, or it's hidden,
as if you'd been wrong to believe in loss.
And some days the emptiness
of the sky looks so immaculate
you think you can just step off
into it and feel one explanation
giving way to another,
and see beneath you
everyone gazing up and crying out.

Twelfth Night

In the middle of the path not far from your house
you find a letter. You never suspect
it's a trick. You're that trusting,
that easily deceived. You don't even hear
the schemers whooping and sniggering

a few feet away in the garden, because this isn't
the real world, it's a play in which a man
needs about five seconds to fall in love
with a girl he thought was a boy since the hour
they first met. Does he really want to be with a boy?
He doesn't think about it. Love is madness,

and then you get married. Desire is madness
as well, but that gets you locked up
in a dark room where you can howl and cry out
that you've been abused. Which is true.
Your part in all this is to be made fun of

by fools and drunkards. It's a comedy.
Nobody dies. Everyone is given
what looks to them like happiness,
except you. Still, there's that moment
when you open the letter
and read it aloud, overwhelmed to discover

how much you're beloved. At the end
your bitterness becomes part of the scheme
that ties almost everything together.
Let the lovers go plan their weddings.
Someone has to want what he'll never have.

Afraid

We knew that he did certain things,
they said of the man they'd just killed,
and all these things in fact happened
when he arrived at the house and went inside.
Then the ones who escaped replied,

Our credibility comes when our leaders
are killed. And they added:
Those of us who die, go to heaven.
Those of you who die, go to hell.

Then the weather got worse—hot, humid,
the air clogged with pollen. Someone said,
It's like we're underwater. Global warming,
someone else suggested, but we understood
that simplified the issue.

No one important had been assassinated
so far that day. At least we hadn't been told.
But everywhere people were doing things
others knew about, or could predict.
After lunch, I lay down on the couch

with a book, and fell into the kind of half-
sleep that's exhausting and involved
dreams that feel like thinking but aren't.
In one a dog attacked my dog, and I shot it.

Now my neighbor's starting up his lawnmower.
He just likes to ride around making noise,
and I'd let my mind follow him
toward the ditch he might drive into
but I've done that before. I've imagined worse.

Most of us don't kill our neighbors,
but some of us do. Write about what
you're afraid of, Donald Barthelme once
told his students. I'd like to go back

and ask what advice he'd give them now.
Write about what makes you happy,
he might say. Both kinds of thinking
will take you to the same place.

Is this a good life? someone asks.
There are slices of melon on the table.
A glass of water and an orange.
Glittering wire along the barricades.

Little Bird

One cloud was following another
across a blue and passionless sky.
It was the middle of summer, far enough
from December for a man to feel indifferent
to the memories of cold, not yet close
enough to autumn to be caught up
in all its folderol about death.
Neither cloud looked like a whale
or a weasel, or any kind of fanciful beast.
All morning I'd felt my life dragging me down.
The view from my window refused to lift my heart.
The sight of a blank piece of paper
filled me with sadness. I wanted to set
my life down in a comfortable chair, tell it
to take a long nap, and walk away as if
I were somebody else, somebody without a house
or a family or a job, but somebody who might
soon feel with a pang precisely the absence
of everything I had. A cool breeze lifted
the curtains in the room where I was sitting.
A bird was singing, nearby
but out of sight. Had it been singing for long?
Far off there were mountains, but I didn't
wish to go there. Nor did I yearn
to be standing by a lake, or walking
beside the tumult of the sea.
The little bird kept repeating its song.
I filled a glass with water and watched it tremble.

The Hero's Luck

When something bad happens
we play it back in our minds,
looking for a place to step in
and change things. We should go outside
right now, you might have said. Or:
Let's not drive anywhere today.

The sea rises, the mountain collapses.
A car swerves toward the crowd
you've just led your family into.
We all look for reasons. Luck
isn't the word you want to hear.
What happened had to,

or it didn't. Maybe
the exceptional man can change direction
in midair, thread the needle's eye,
and come out whole. But even the hero
who stands up to chance has to feel
how far the world will bend

until it breaks him. He can see
that day: the unappeasable ocean,
the cascades of stone. A crowd
gathers around his body. He sees that too.
Someone is saying: His luck just ran out.
It happens to us all.

Nothing There

What would make you happier?
was the question, and I was surprised
24% chose "more meaning in your life,"
as if the problem was how much of it
they didn't have. Of course
they were asking for meaning that helps,
the kind that gives us good reasons
for loss—a child dies, love fades, then friendship,
and soon enough almost everything is gone.

"Why can't we just live terrified
and without consolation?" my friend Stephen said.
"That's how I like it." What he really liked
was saying it that way, the little shock
of embracing fear, of going out to meet
what most of us try hard to avoid. And that
reminded me of the story David used to tell
when we were in college. His car breaks down
or runs out of gas so he finds himself walking

alone, at night, on an empty road, silence
deepening all around, and very soon
he's certain something's following him. He stops,
it stops. To his left: cornfields. And then
quite suddenly he surprises himself
by rushing into them, is surprised even more
when, convinced it's gaining on him,
he turns back, relieved, even glad
to surrender. And of course

it's not there, though that cornfield
must have been spooky enough
in the moonlight, a little breeze

moving the shadows around, those papery husks
scraping against each other. In the end,
embarrassment. Then a story. His point
was what you could do to yourself
just by thinking. Or maybe
that wasn't his point. It's been years,

and for reasons I don't understand, perhaps
for no reason at all, our friendship
was set aside, as if nothing had been there
to begin with, the way nothing
was out in that field. Or else
it chose to hide—at the moment
David turned to give himself up—slipping back
into the rows of dry corn, satisfied
to have done whatever it had done.

Isn't It About Time

something extraordinary happened?
—not to me personally, but something
large and important for us all,
like the return of our smarter ancestors,
the ones who migrated, eons ago,

to an alternate universe, where they
sat around their sleek uncomplicated quarters
and watched us fuck up our lives until
they knew they had to come back to earth
because we weren't going to make it on our own.

That's one way of thinking about salvation.
But those wise aliens never look much different
from the mean ones who are planning
on wiping us out, in which case our story
is all about triumphant battles or pure dumb luck

and isn't that too much like the world
we're stuck in already?
Then there's God, who still understands
we want to be told what to do
even when we say we can't bear it anymore.

It's June. The window's open. Outside
in the dark a few frogs have started
calling to each other, back and forth
in a design as clear
and symmetrical as any fairy tale.

I want the ending where I'm tucked into bed.
I want God to set his glass of water
on my nightstand, and when he steps away
leave the light on in the hall
until I close my eyes and sleep takes over.

The Reason Being

If I play Tchaikovsky I play his melodies and
skip his spiritual struggles. . . . I have to know
just how many notes my audience will stand for.
—LIBERACE

As soon as you hear it you know
it's a melody, and that's what you want.
Moreover, you don't have to understand
anything to like it, nothing about scales
or keys, nothing about history

or the difficult life of the composer,
the women or men he loved or couldn't love,
how much money he didn't have, how cold
it would get when he tried to compose,
how he died. These are some of the things

you don't have to know because the melody
is like a small bird, maybe a yellow canary,
that wings its way into your mind
—no, into your heart—
where there's a perch already

set up for it, a little trapeze
to swing back and forth on as it sings
and sings, since a good melody
stays with you, sometimes much longer
than you'd like, the reason being

the relatively small number of notes.
And these can repeat and repeat until you
have to replace them with another melody,
shoo that bird away, so to speak, invite
a different one in. Or else go to sleep.

But even then the melody can wake you,
or start up in your dreams, no longer
that pretty bird now but something shapeless
and troubled, something struggling,
but why, or with what, you don't know.

Hurricane Season

June 2007

After Jenny fell out of love with Sam
she fell in love with Asher. How difficult
was the time in between? On a scale of one
to ten at least an eight, during which
we all learned how little satisfaction
you can get out of blame. The many ways
we're lied to every day by those in control
of our lives make it amazing that anyone
can lay a hand on someone else and hope
it will feel like tenderness. Or perhaps
the private life is what we've retreated to
as our country slides deeper into disgrace.
Have we become so fragile every word
is the right word only if spoken
just so? Does "I'll call you tomorrow"
mean tomorrow? Does "Of course" mean maybe?
Hurricane season is beginning and we've
been told what to expect. I remember
Kurt Vonnegut saying, "Everything is going
to get a lot worse and never get any better,"
and that was years ago. How do we make
all this look like someone else's fault?
is what our president is wondering.
How can I avoid doing anything? Soon
one of those storms we can only expect more of
assembles into red and yellow blotches
on the Doppler screen. Rotation is possible.
Damaging winds. Nickel-size hail.
When Sam tried to kill himself Jenny discovered
how she'd been deceived and she understood
they couldn't go on. You can live for years

with someone you think you know and then
you don't. You can lie so brazenly
to the country you're in charge of that millions
are convinced you're sincere. "This will certainly
teach me a lesson," is what Vonnegut said
the condemned prisoner's last words should be.
Who can doubt the bitterness of our future?—
unless you're counting on being raptured away
or have already planned to blow yourself up
to earn your place in heaven. Ten minutes
of furious rain and this storm is over.
Thursday another front will pass through.
When Jenny fell out of love with Sam she thought
she'd never be in love again and I said,
Yes, you will, and sooner than you think,
which was easy for me to say because
I was her father and I believed it,
though I'd have said the same thing
even if I hadn't known it was the truth.

Adam's Dream

In his dream a few of the animals
had been left unnamed.
He could see them grazing

safely in a separate field,
never wandering very far
from that place, or each other.

He'd been told naming them
was his job, that was the way
he could own them. And in fact

he'd completed his task.
Why, then, should he return
in his sleep just to watch them?

Was this what he wanted—to keep
some part of the world a secret?
Beyond himself, beyond God?

Gratitude

"I pressed something and you went away,"
I was saying after we got reconnected,
though I hadn't figured out which button
made that happen. At your end

the rain was over. "Rebecca says
it's cold," you said, "but you don't notice
it's cold because it's so humid."
In the old days it made sense not to talk

for weeks or months. Sometimes we wrote letters,
which doesn't mean that was a better time
or a richer life. I like knowing the weather
in Boston right now, and what you're planning

to cook for dinner, and who's ahead
in the important match. "England just made
a *fantastic* save," you explain, as the little
device I'm holding against my ear

keeps getting warmer. Didn't someone
warn us about cell phones and cancer?
Was that ever cleared up? Where I was
it should have been raining but wasn't,

and I wish I'd taken that as good luck
and not the kind of moment just before
the next bad thing happens. I tell you
I've decided not to read the papers because

I don't want to know what new advances
the bird flu is making, or how many were killed
yesterday in Baghdad and Kabul. How guilty
should I feel for trying to stay uninformed?

I can hear the game behind your voice,
the pause when something exciting happens.
"That was close," you say, as if I weren't
hundreds of miles off, watching the sky

getting hazier and hazier, and wondering
if there isn't a way to exchange
feeling nervous about everything
for some kind of gratitude.

The Weed Whacker Makes Me Yearn for the Scythe

and all the other instruments of silence,
lawns mowed by sheep, for example,
their soft eyes fixed on the earth,
the small sounds of their labor never rising
to the upper floors of some vast country house
where, centuries ago, I'm hard at work
on a new poem for my patron. Right now

I'm distracted by the extravagant view,
which reminds me of the many consolations
of great wealth, although my subject
this morning is neither privilege
nor pleasure, but time—his choice,
following yesterday's underappreciated ode
on virtue. Tell me, he said, what you think
I should feel, and I wanted to suggest

how much more inspiring I would find
a slightly larger room, one farther away
from the servants, and their whispering.
Ah, the wanton hours—they turn, they laugh! No,
personification irritates him. I must be wary
of the sea itself, restless and unfathomable,
though birds in flight may work, even those sheep

whose ceaseless munching I've been trying
all morning not to imagine. *The scythe
glides silently through the bending grass.*
Or should it be wheat? Yet always it glides.
And clouds pass, as all things will
in this world, I might add, but do not, since death
pleases him only if the thought of it
reminds someone pretty how foolish she is

to cherish that which worms too soon
will take without asking. A good point,
he'll tell me later, perhaps noting
that "the soft eyes of sheep" strikes him
as unnecessary—too poetic, or else too common,
like the unmown fields, or the scythe
some weary laborer has left gleaming
out there in the noonday sun.

Notes

"Hawthorne on His Way Home": "A person to be writing a tale, and to find that it shapes itself against his intentions; that the characters act otherwise than he thought; that unforeseen events occur; and a catastrophe comes which he strives in vain to avert. It might shadow forth his own fate,—he having made himself one of the personages."
—Nathaniel Hawthorne, *The American Notebooks*

"According to Freud": The title and first line are borrowed from Dean Young's poem, "I Am But a Traveler in This Land & Know Little of Its Ways."

"The Origin of Surrealism": "Let us not mince words: the astonishing is always beautiful, anything astonishing is beautiful, in fact nothing but the astonishing is beautiful." —André Breton, "Manifesto of Surrealism" (1924)

"Once Something Must Have Happened Here": The title is borrowed from the first line of "Spectacular" by Meghan O'Rourke.

"Murdercycle": *Murdercycle* is an actual movie (and the quote from *TV Guide* is genuine). The plot of the poem, however, is entirely invented, even though it is indebted to the whole genre of films that feature possessed vehicles, especially *Killdozer* and *The Car* (also more excitingly known as *DeathMobile*).

"Afraid": The final stanza borrows some gestures from the first paragraph of Donald Barthelme's wonderful story "The Indian Uprising": "We defended the city as best we could. The arrows of the Comanches came in clouds. The war clubs of the Comanches clattered on the soft, yellow pavements. There were earthworks along the Boulevard Mark Clark and the hedges had been laced with sparkling wire. People were trying to understand. I spoke to Sylvia. 'Do you think this is a good life?' The table held apples, books, long-playing records. She looked up. 'No.'"

Lawrence Raab is the author of six previous collections of poems, including *Visible Signs: New and Selected Poems* (Penguin, 2003), *The Probable World* (Penguin, 2000), and *What We Don't Know About Each Other* (Penguin, 1993), a winner of the National Poetry Series and a finalist for the National Book Award. He has received grants from the National Endowment for the Arts, the Mellon Foundation, the Massachusetts Council on the Arts, and the Guggenheim Foundation. He teaches literature and writing at Williams College.

JOHN ASHBERY
Selected Poems
Self-Portrait in a Convex
  Mirror

TED BERRIGAN
The Sonnets

JOE BONOMO
Installations

PHILIP BOOTH
Selves

JIM CARROLL
Fear of Dreaming: The Selected
  Poems
Living at the Movies
Void of Course

ALISON HAWTHORNE DEMING
Genius Loci

CARL DENNIS
New and Selected Poems
  1974–2004
Practical Gods
Ranking the Wishes
Unknown Friends

DIANE DI PRIMA
Loba

STUART DISCHELL
Backwards Days
Dig Safe

STEPHEN DOBYNS
Velocities: New and
  Selected Poems,
  1966–1992

EDWARD DORN
Way More West: New and
  Selected Poems

AMY GERSTLER
Crown of Weeds
Ghost Girl
Medicine
Nerve Storm

EUGENE GLORIA
Drivers at the Short-Time
  Motel
Hoodlum Birds

DEBORA GREGER
Desert Fathers, Uranium
  Daughters
God
Men, Women, and Ghosts
Western Art

TERRANCE HAYES
Hip Logic
Wind in a Box

ROBERT HUNTER
Sentinel and Other Poems

MARY KARR
Viper Rum

WILLIAM KECKLER
Sanskrit of the Body

JACK KEROUAC
Book of Sketches
Book of Blues
Book of Haikus

JOANNA KLINK
Circadian

JOANNE KYGER
As Ever: Selected Poems

ANN LAUTERBACH
Hum
If In Time: Selected Poems,
  1975–2000
On a Stair
Or to Begin Again

CORINNE LEE
PYX

PHILLIS LEVIN
May Day
Mercury

WILLIAM LOGAN
Macbeth in Venice
Strange Flesh
The Whispering Gallery

MICHAEL MCCLURE
Huge Dreams: San Francisco
  and Beat Poems

DAVID MELTZER
David's Copy: The Selected
  Poems of David Meltzer

CAROL MUSKE
An Octave above Thunder
Red Trousseau

ALICE NOTLEY
The Descent of Alette
Disobedience
In the Pines
Mysteries of Small Houses

LAWRENCE RAAB
Visible Signs: New and
  Selected Poems

BARBARA RAS
One Hidden Stuff

PATTIANN ROGERS
Generations
Wayfare

WILLIAM STOBB
Nervous Systems

TRYFON TOLIDES
An Almost Pure Empty
  Walking

ANNE WALDMAN
Kill or Cure
Manatee/Humanity
Structure of the World
  Compared to a Bubble

JAMES WELCH
Riding the Earthboy 40

PHILIP WHALEN
Overtime: Selected Poems

ROBERT WRIGLEY
Earthly Meditations: New and
  Selected Poems
Lives of the Animals
Reign of Snakes

MARK YAKICH
The Importance of Peeling
  Potatoes in Ukraine
Unrelated Individuals
  Forming a Group Waiting
  to Cross

JOHN YAU
Borrowed Love Poems
Paradiso Diaspora